# MINERALS

Patricia Miller-Schroeder

MEDIA ENHANCED BOOKS
AV2
BY WEIGL
ADDED VALUE • AUDIO VISUAL

www.av2books.com

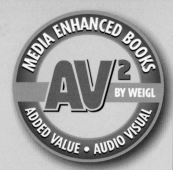

**BOOK CODE**

S917135

AV² **by Weigl** brings you media enhanced books that support active learning.

AV² provides enriched content that supplements and complements this book. Weigl's AV² books strive to create inspired learning and engage young minds for a total learning experience.

Go to **www.av2books.com**, and enter this book's unique code. You will have access to video, audio, web links, quizzes, a slide show, and activities.

**Audio**
Listen to sections of the book read aloud.

**Video**
Watch informative video clips.

**Web Link**
Find research sites and play interactive games.

**Try This!**
Complete activities and hands-on experiments.

Due to the dynamic nature of the Internet, some of the URLs and activities provided as part of AV² by Weigl may have changed or ceased to exist. AV² by Weigl accepts no responsibility for any such changes. All media enhanced books are regularly monitored to update addresses and sites in a timely manner. Contact AV² by Weigl at 1-866-64-WEIGL or av2books@weigl.com with any questions, comments, or feedback.

Published by AV² by Weigl
350 5th Avenue, 59th Floor
New York, NY 10118
Website: www.av2books.com    www.weigl.com

Library of Congress Cataloging-in-Publication Data

Miller-Schroeder, Patricia.
 Minerals / Patricia Miller-Schroeder.
   p. cm. -- (Earth science)
Includes index.
ISBN 978-1-60596-976-3 (hardcover : alk. paper) -- ISBN 978-1-60596-977-0 (softcover : alk. paper) -- ISBN 978-1-60596-978-7 (e-book)
1. Minerals--Juvenile literature. I. Title.
 QE365.2.M552 2010
 549--dc22
                          2009050238

Printed in the United States of America in North Mankato, Minnesota
1 2 3 4 5 6 7 8 9 0  14 13 12 11 10

052010
WEP264000

Project Coordinator: Heather C. Hudak
Design: Terry Paulhus

Photo Credits
Every reasonable effort has been made to trace ownership and to obtain permission to reprint copyright material. The publishers would be pleased to have any errors or omissions brought to their attention so that they may be corrected in subsequent printings.

Weigl acknowledges Getty Images as its primary image supplier for this title.

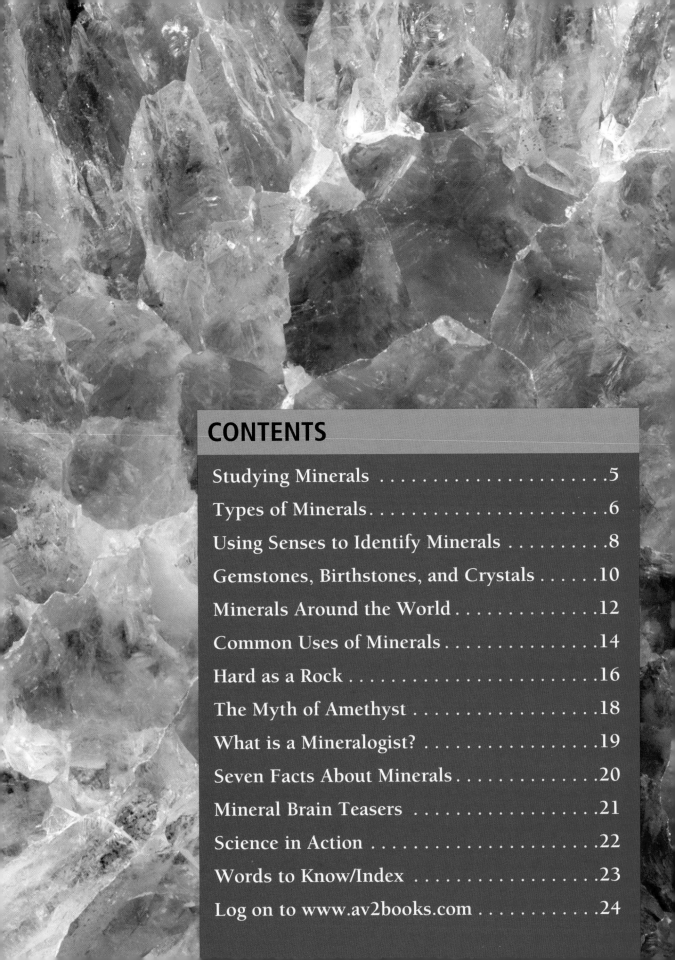

# CONTENTS

Gold is valuable because it is rare. In the 1800s, many people traveled to places such as California and the Yukon in Canada in search of gold. Most people looking for gold during this period did so by sifting through river rocks. Today, most gold is mined. Some is mined in open pits, which can cause a great deal of harm to the local environment.

# Studying Minerals

Minerals are solid materials that are found in the natural environment. They are made of materials that were never alive. Minerals are all around us. The salt we put on food is a mineral. The sand on beaches is a mineral. Cars, buses, and bicycles are made of minerals. There are even minerals in our bodies. Minerals are the most common materials on Earth.

Minerals are found in space as well as on Earth. Minerals have been found on planets, moons, and **meteorites**. Some minerals are rare and expensive. They are called gemstones. Gemstones are usually shaped, polished, and placed in jewelry. Diamonds are often used in wedding rings and expensive jewelry. Gold, for example, always contains small amounts of other metals such as silver, copper, and iron.

■ Scientists have discovered more than 3,000 different minerals. Only about 100 of them are very common, but all are very useful.

# Types of Minerals

All the rocks, pebbles, and sand on Earth are formed out of minerals. However, not every mineral forms a rock. Minerals and rocks are made of **elements**. A few minerals are made of only one element. These minerals are called native elements. They include gold, copper, silver, and carbon.

## SILICATES

- Are the largest group of minerals
- Created when metals mix with silicon and oxygen
- Outnumber all the other minerals put together
- Include mica, which often shines in rocks, topaz, a pretty gemstone, and talc, which is the softest mineral

## OXIDES

- Made when metal is affected by oxygen
- Some, such as bauxite, are mined. Bauxite is used to make aluminum. Corundum, another oxide mineral, is very hard and sharp. It is used to make sandpaper.
- Can be gems, such as rubies and sapphires

## HALIDES

- Made from halogen elements, such as chlorine, bromine, fluorine, and iodine, mixed with metallic elements
- Are very soft and can be dissolved by water
- Salt is a well-known mineral in this group.

All minerals are made up of more than one element. These are called complex minerals. Pyrite, a shiny mineral that is also called "fool's gold," is a complex mineral. It is made of iron and sulfur. Pyrite is called "fool's gold" because it has a similar appearance, but is not as valuable. Quartz, beryl, and talc are other complex minerals.

## CARBONATES

- A group of minerals made of carbon, oxygen, and a metallic element
- Examples include calcite, aragonite, and marble.
- Calcite is one of the most common minerals on Earth. It forms crystals of many different colors and shapes.

## SULFIDES

- Are made of mixtures of sulfur and metals
- Are are usually heavy and break easily
- Examples include pyrites, such as iron ore, arsenic, antimony, and cinnabar, which is used to make quicksilver mercury, the main ingredient in a thermometer.

## OTHER KINDS

- Includes sulfates, phosphates, and native elements
- Sulfate minerals are often soft and transparent.
- Phosphates, such as turquoise, are often brightly colored.
- Native elements may include diamonds, gold, and **graphite**.

# Using Senses to Identify Minerals

Scientists use their senses of sight, smell, and taste to identify minerals. Some minerals are known for their color. Malachite is green, and azurite is blue. The mineral halite can be identified by taste. This mineral is commonly known as table salt.

The **properties** of some minerals can be seen just by looking at them. Some minerals have a unique color. Others have a distinctive shine. Minerals even leave special marks that allow them to be easily identified.

■ Some minerals have a distinct odor. Sulfur is a mineral that smells like rotten eggs.

One of the easiest mineral properties to identify is color. Many minerals have rich colors, ranging from deep red to bright yellow. However, colors are not always the best way to identify minerals. Many minerals come in several different colors.

**Luster** is another property that can be seen in a mineral. Some minerals, such as pyrite, shine brightly under light. Other minerals are quite dull.

Streak is the color a mineral leaves when it is rubbed on a special tile. The color of the streak may be different from the mineral's color, but the color of the streak is always the same for that mineral.

## MINERAL STREAK COLORS

| | Mineral | Color | Streak |
|---|---|---|---|
| | Biotite | brown to brownish black | brown-gray |
| | Chlorite | green or blackish green | green-yellow |
| | Cinnabar | reddish black | red-brown |
| | Hematite | silver-gray | red-brown |
| | Hornblende | black | green-gray |
| | Pyrite | gold or brass | greenish black to black |
| | Olivine | green | white |
| | Garnet | deep red, sometimes green | white |

# Gemstones, Birthstones, and Crystals

Gemstones are minerals that have been cut and polished. They are often crystals with rich, vivid colors. The most valuable gemstones are also rare.

Gemstones have been used to represent the months of the year. This has been a custom for thousands of years. Certain gems are worn to indicate the month of a person's birth. These gems are called birthstones. The gemstones that represent each month have varied in different times and places.

■ Quartz crystals are named for their color. Amethyst is purple quartz.

Look at grains of sand, salt, or sugar using a magnifying glass or **microscope**. You will see that they are made up of tiny crystals. Crystals are solid substances with a pattern of flat surfaces called faces.

Each mineral has its own crystal pattern. This is like a person's fingerprint. Every person's fingerprint is unique. It is the same for minerals. No two minerals have the same pattern. Scientists can tell what mineral they are looking at by examining its crystal pattern.

## Birthstone Chart

This chart shows the birthstones for each month of the year.

| January | February | March | April |
|---|---|---|---|
| garnet | amethyst | aquamarine | diamond |
| **May** | **June** | **July** | **August** |
| emerald | pearl | ruby | peridot |
| **September** | **October** | **November** | **December** |
| sapphire | opal | topaz | turquoise |

# Minerals Around the World

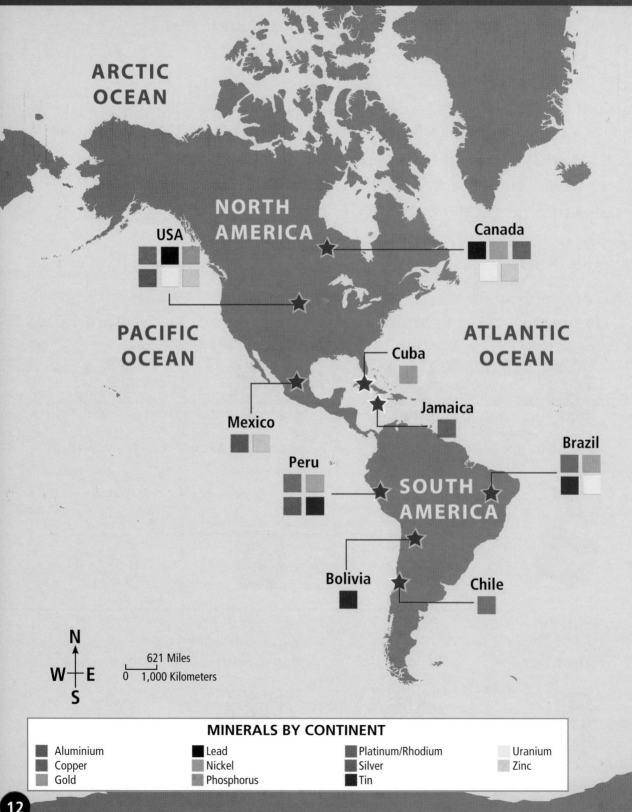

ARCTIC OCEAN

NORTH AMERICA

USA

Canada

PACIFIC OCEAN

ATLANTIC OCEAN

Cuba

Jamaica

Mexico

Brazil

Peru

SOUTH AMERICA

Bolivia

Chile

N
W — E
S

621 Miles
0   1,000 Kilometers

### MINERALS BY CONTINENT

| | | | | | | | |
|---|---|---|---|---|---|---|---|
| ■ Aluminium | | ■ Lead | | ■ Platinum/Rhodium | | ■ Uranium | |
| ■ Copper | | ■ Nickel | | ■ Silver | | ■ Zinc | |
| ■ Gold | | ■ Phosphorus | | ■ Tin | | | |

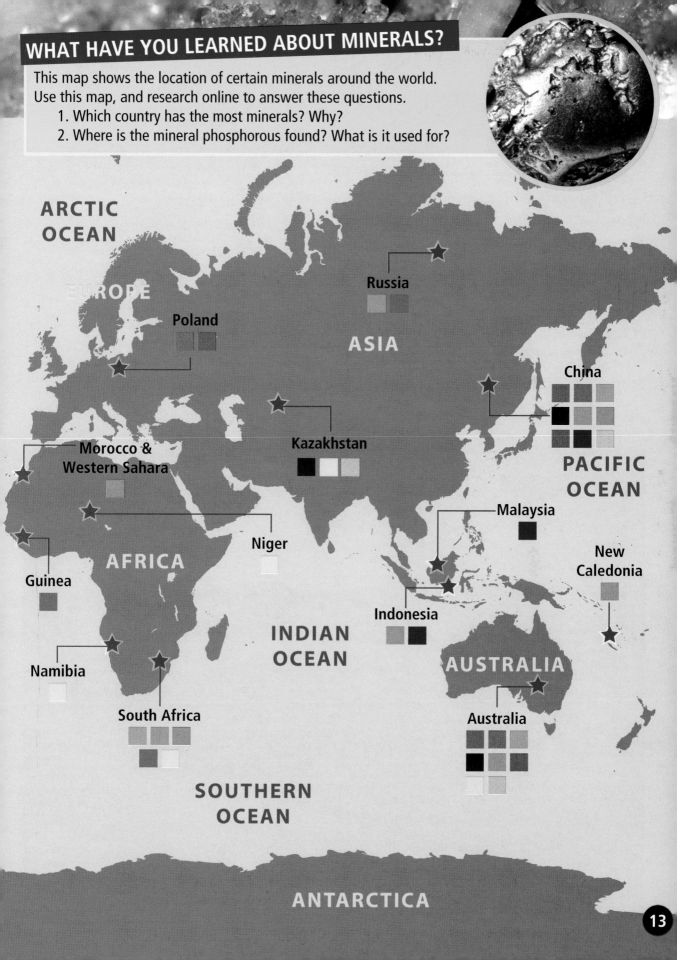

# WHAT HAVE YOU LEARNED ABOUT MINERALS?

This map shows the location of certain minerals around the world. Use this map, and research online to answer these questions.

1. Which country has the most minerals? Why?
2. Where is the mineral phosphorous found? What is it used for?

ARCTIC OCEAN

EUROPE

ASIA

Russia

Poland

China

Morocco & Western Sahara

Kazakhstan

PACIFIC OCEAN

Malaysia

AFRICA

Niger

New Caledonia

Guinea

Namibia

Indonesia

INDIAN OCEAN

AUSTRALIA

South Africa

Australia

SOUTHERN OCEAN

ANTARCTICA

# Common Uses of Minerals

Minerals are used to make parts of many everyday objects. Quartz is one of the most common minerals. It is found in many kinds of rocks all around the world. Quartz is used to make glass, watch parts, electronic equipment, and many other things.

Gypsum is another common mineral. It is used in cement, toothpaste, crayons, and bakery products. Copper is used in coins, electrical wire, pipes, and airbags.

■ A telephone contains more than 40 different minerals, a television set has about 35, and an automobile has about 15.

Diamonds are some of the most valuable minerals. Diamonds are used in some of the most expensive jewelry in the world. They are also the hardest mineral. They are valuable in drill bits, saws, and other tools because of their **hardness**. Diamond **scalpels** are used in surgery.

Halite, or salt, is another valuable mineral. The bodies of humans and animals need salt to stay healthy. Salt is used in baking, in **salt licks** for animals, and to flavor foods. It is also used to preserve food and keep it from spoiling. Salt has been used as a form of money in many countries. Soldiers in ancient Rome were paid with salt—a salarium. The word "salary" comes from this Roman word.

■ About 65 percent of the world's diamonds come from countries in Africa.

# Hard as a Rock

Some minerals are harder than others. In 1822, Friedrich Mohs invented a way to test mineral hardness. He used 10 common minerals and developed the Mohs scale. The scale rates minerals in order of hardness from one for softest to ten for hardest. Mohs rated the minerals by testing which ones could scratch the others. Now, any mineral can be tested using this scale.

Minerals that are low on the scale can be scratched with a fingernail. Minerals high on the scale are harder to scratch. Diamonds have a hardness of 10. They cannot be scratched by any other mineral. They can, however, scratch everything else.

■ Coal is a very valuable mineral. It is made from the remains of vast swamps and forests that covered much of the world more than 300 million years ago.

Coal burns well, and more is used today than ever before in history, mostly for generating power. Coal mining in the United States is often done by removing the top layer of rock from an entire mountain. This destroys countless plants and animals, and pollutes nearby water. Saving energy at home can reduce the need for coal and help stop this environmentally harmful practice.

# THE MOHS SCALE OF HARDNESS

| 10 | Diamond | Scratches all other minerals |
| 9 | Corundum | Cuts glass |
| 8 | Topaz | Scratches glass easily |
| 7 | Quartz | Not scratched by a **file** |
| 6 | Feldspar | Cannot be scratched with a knife but scratches glass with difficulty |
| 5 | Apatite | Scratched with a knife with difficulty |
| 4 | Fluorite | Not scratched by a copper coin; does not scratch glass |
| 3 | Calcite | Scratches and is scratched by a copper coin |
| 2 | Gypsum | Just scratched by a fingernail |
| 1 | Talc | Easily scratched by a fingernail |

# The Myth of Amethyst

In ancient times, people created stories to explain how certain things were created. These stories were called myths. Many well-known myths are from ancient Greece. One myth explains how the mineral amethyst was created.

Bacchus, the god of wine, was angry one day. He said the next person who walked by would be eaten by his tigers. A young woman named Amethyst was the next person to pass Bacchus. The goddess Diana saved her from being eaten by turning her into a white stone.

Bacchus was sorry for what he had done. He poured wine over the white stone, giving the stone a purple hue. That is how amethyst got its color and name.

■ Amethyst turns from purple to a dull yellow when it is heated.

# What is a Mineralogist?

People who study minerals are called mineralogists. Mineralogists learn where minerals are found and how they form. They learn how to identify different minerals by learning mineral properties.

Mineralogists often work for governments, universities, or mining companies. Others work in laboratories studying rock and soil samples. Some mineralogists even study minerals in space.

## Friedrich Mohs

Friedrich Mohs was a well-known German mineralogist who lived from 1773 to 1839. In 1801, Mohs moved to Austria and was hired by a rich banker to identify the banker's valuable mineral collection. During this job, Mohs came up with a way of scraping minerals against one another to find out what they were. This led to his invention of the Mohs Scale of Hardness in 1812, a scale that is still used today by many mineralogists.

## EQUIPMENT

Mineralogists use powerful electron microscopes and **x-rays**. With these tools, mineralogists can see the inner structure of minerals.

Mineralogists use rock hammers and picks to remove minerals from the ground. They look at the minerals with magnifying lenses. Sometimes, they put the mineral samples in a collecting bag to take back to the laboratory.

Rock Hammer

# Seven Facts
# About Minerals

Calcium is a mineral that is needed by the body. It keeps teeth and bones healthy, and lets the body absorb nutrients.

Gold is a mineral that can be hammered into many shapes. One ounce (29 grams) of gold can be shaped into a wire 62 miles (100 kilometers) long.

Liquid water is not a mineral, but frozen water is. When water freezes and becomes ice crystals and snowflakes, minerals form.

The amount of gold found on Earth, through all time, would fill two Olympic swimming pools.

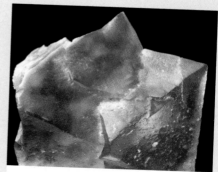

Fluorite is the second most popular mineral for mineral collectors. Only quartz is more popular.

The most common mineral on Earth is quartz.

Plants, animals, and humans need minerals to live.

# Mineral Brain Teasers

**1** What is the colored mark a mineral leaves on a special tile called?

**2** What does the mineral sulfur smell like?

**3** What is pyrite sometimes called?

**4** What does the Mohs scale measure?

**5** What is copper used to make?

**6** What are scientists who study minerals called?

**7** What is the hardest mineral?

**8** What are minerals that are made from only one element called?

**9** Name two types of tools that mineralogists use in their work?

**10** True or false? Your body needs minerals to live and stay healthy.

**ANSWERS:** 1. Streak 2. Rotten eggs 3. Fool's gold 4. Hardness 5. Copper is used to make coins, electrical wire, and pipes. 6. Mineralogists 7. Diamond 8. Native elements 9. Any two of electron microscopes, x-rays, magnifying lenses, rock hammers, picks, and collecting bags. 10. True

21

# Science in Action

## Growing Crystals

Crystals form in several ways. One way is when minerals and rocks that melted deep under Earth's surface cool. You can see how simple crystals form by using water, a string, and sugar.

## Tools Needed

Spoon      String      Sugar      Water      Food coloring

## Directions

**1** Cut a piece of string that is slightly shorter than the glass. Tie the string to the pencil.

**2** With an adult's help, boil some water.

**3** Dissolve several spoons of sugar in the hot water. When no more sugar will dissolve, dangle a string in the water. To color the crystals, add a few drops of food coloring to the water, and stir.

**4** Fill the glass with boiling water.

**5** Lay the pencil across the top of the glass so that the string is dangling inside the glass. Make sure the string does not touch the sides or bottom of the glass.

**6** Put the glass in a safe place where it will not be moved. After one day, check if you can see the crystals growing. When the crystals are done growing, pull the string out of the water, and allow them to dry.

**7** As the sugar water cools, sugar crystals will form on the string. This will take a long time. Layers of crystals will build up and continue to grow.

22

# Words to Know

**elements**: basic matter that cannot be broken down any further

**file**: a metal tool with ridges on one or both sides used to cut, smooth, or grind hard surfaces

**graphite**: a soft mineral used for pencil lead

**hardness**: ability of a mineral to resist being scratched

**luster**: amount of shine a mineral has under a bright light

**meteorites**: rocks or metals that fall to Earth from space

**microscope**: a tool used to magnify and study very small objects

**properties**: characteristics or qualities

**salt licks**: deposits or blocks of salt that animals, especially cattle, deer, and sheep, regularly lick

**scalpels**: straight knives used in surgery

**x-rays**: special photographs taken with beams that can show what is inside a rock

# Index

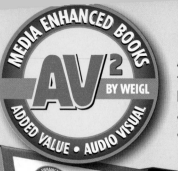

# Log on to www.av2books.com

AV² by Weigl brings you media enhanced books that support active learning. Go to **www.av2books.com**, and enter the special code inside the front cover of this book. You will gain access to enriched and enhanced content that supplements and complements this book. Content includes video, audio, web links, quizzes, a slide show, and activities.

**Audio**
Listen to sections of the book read aloud.

**Video**
Watch informative video clips.

**Web Link**
Find research sites and play interactive games.

**Try This!**
Complete activities and hands-on experiments.

# WHAT'S ONLINE?

**Try This!**
Complete activities and hands-on experiments.

**Pages 6-7** Complete an activity about types of minerals.

**Pages 12-13** See if you can identify minerals around the world.

**Pages 16-17** Try an activity on Mohs Scale of Hardness.

**Pages 18-19** Write about a day in the life of a mineralogist.

**Page 22** Try the activity in the book, then play an interactive game.

**Web Link**
Find research sites and play interactive games.

**Pages 8-9** Link to more information about identifying minerals.

**Pages 10-11** Find out more about gemstones, birthstones, and crystals.

**Pages 18-19** Learn more about being a mineralogist.

**Page 20** Link to facts about minerals.

**Video**
Watch informative video clips.

**Pages 4-5** Watch a video about minerals.

**Pages 14-15** Learn more about common uses for minerals.

**EXTRA FEATURES**

**Audio**
Hear introductory audio at the top of every page

**Key Words**
Study vocabulary, and play a matching word game.

**Slide Show**
View images and captions, and try a writing activity.

**AV² Quiz**
Take this quiz to test your knowledge